PRAYING

through the

SANCTUARY

30 Days of Prayer
for Revival and Reformation

Tim Rumsey

PTS-BOOK
ISBN: 978-1-950907-27-4

For more Bible study resources visit www.PathwayToParadise.org.

Contents

Forward 5

Section 1: The Gate 7

Section 2: The Altar of Burnt Offering 17

Section 3: The Laver 27

Section 4: The Table of Shewbread 37

Section 5: The Altar of Incense 47

Section 6: The Candlestick 57

Section 7: The Ark of the Covenant 67

Concluding Prayers.. 77

Forward

"Thy way, O God, is in the sanctuary: who is so great a God as our God? Thou art the God that doest wonders: thou hast declared thy strength among the people."

Psalm 77:13, 14

I still remember sitting in first grade, listening to my teacher sing silly songs about the letters of the alphabet. Her eager troop of young students giggled at the funny stories these impromptu ballads related about vowels getting lost and consonants going in search of them. She also drew a lot of pictures on the chalkboard in an effort to help us visualize and remember the bewildering array of 26 letters. It must have worked, because many decades later I can still see the lonely "e" hanging like an apple from the tree, desperately looking for a word in need of its services.

A good teacher uses symbols, illustrations, and stories to make the point, and to help the lesson stick. God is a good Teacher—the best, in fact—and the Bible identifies the sanctuary as God's grand object lesson of salvation. Every detail of this amazing structure reveals some important aspect of God's perfect plan of salvation. Its layout, construction, furniture, and services all illustrate in vivid and sensory ways the invisible yet ultimately real working of God in human history, and on the individual human heart.

This book focuses on the sanctuary as a divinely-inspired model of prayer. A cycle of four recurring prayers—for yourself, your family, your church, and your community—forms a thirty-day journey beginning at the sanctuary's outer gate and finishing in the Most Holy Place. I pray that you will find fresh inspiration and motivation for prayer as you pray through the sanctuary, seeking God's blessings and claiming His promises. Enjoy the journey!

Tim Rumsey
Speaker/Director, Pathway to Paradise Ministries

The Gate

"Then said Jesus unto them again, Verily, verily, I say unto you, I am the door of the sheep.

John 10:7

The wilderness sanctuary erected by Moses and the Israelites during their sojourn in the desert contained only one gate, situated on the east side of the courtyard. The gate was made of linen, which was dyed blue, red, and purple. The color blue represented the law of God, while red pointed forward to the Messiah's blood shed to pay the penalty of death required by that law. The color purple—a mixture of red and blue—symbolized royalty and the promise of adoption into God's royal family for all who accepted Jesus Christ as their personal Savior and Lord. Both then and now, the gate represents Jesus Christ and His work of redemption for sinful humanity.

Day 1

Prayer for Myself

"Behold, I stand at the door, and knock: if any man hear my voice, and open the door, I will come in to him, and will sup with him, and he with me."

Revelation 3:20

The Bible presents Jesus as a gentleman knocking on the doors of our hearts, asking for admittance into our lives, but never forcing His way in. It is comforting to know that God desires a closer relationship with us; however, it is also sobering to realize that the Bible pictures Jesus as standing outside of our hearts—an indication of the separation caused by sin. Many things can cause us to ignore and reject Christ's desire to come into our lives. Fear, pride, selfishness, and materialism are just a few of the roadblocks that often prevent us from opening the doors of our hearts to Jesus. Many people are led to believe that if they give their lives to Jesus, they will lose their freedom, independence, and joy in life; however, the Bible promises that true freedom, individuality, and joy come only through a saving relationship with Jesus Christ. According to the Bible, this is the only path to salvation. Pray today that God will help you open—completely—the door of your heart to Jesus Christ.

Sample Prayer

Dear Jesus, thank You for knocking on the door of my heart. I confess that I have too often responded to You with stubbornness, pride, and disinterest. Please forgive me for these sins, and come into my heart today.

Reflection

_____

_____

_____

_____

_____

_____

_____

Final Thought

The Saviour says, "Behold, I stand at the door, and knock; if any man hear My voice, and open the door, I will come in to him, and will sup with him, and he with Me." Revelation 3:20. He is not repulsed by scorn or turned aside by threatening, but continually seeks the lost ones, saying, "How shall I give thee up?" Hosea 11:8. Although His love is driven back by the stubborn heart, He returns to plead with greater force, "Behold, I stand at the door, and knock." The winning power of His love compels souls to come in. And to Christ they say, "Thy gentleness hath made me great." Psalm 18:35.

Christ's Object Lessons, p. 235

Day 2

Prayer for My Family

"And these words, which I command thee this day, shall be in thine heart: And thou shalt teach them diligently unto thy children, and shalt talk of them when thou sitest in thine house, and when thou walkest by the way, and when thou liest down, and when thou risest up. And thou shalt bind them for a sign upon thine hand, and they shall be as frontlets between thine eyes. And thou shalt write them upon the posts of thy house, and on thy gates."

Deuteronomy 6:6-9

God desires that a wall of protection be placed around every Christian family. That wall of protection is the Word of God. Thousands of years ago, God promised the Israelites that He would bless them and protect them if they wrote His commandments on the doorposts of their homes. It is likely that Israelite families began doing this literally—inscribing the law of God on the posts, beams, and gates of their houses—once they were settled in the land of Canaan, a tradition which continues today. However, this physical inscription of God's Word on a physical structure is meaningless unless His Word has also been written spiritually on the hearts and minds of the occupants. This was, and still is, God's greatest desire—that the principles of love contained in His law be lived out in every family. Pray today that love for God and love toward other people will become living realities in your family!

Sample Prayer

Dear Jesus, please write Your holy law on the minds and hearts of my family, so that we may speak, act, and think in a way that pleases you. Please reveal anything that would prevent You from accomplishing this work in our lives.

Reflection

_____

_____

_____

_____

_____

_____

_____

Final Thought

Had the Israelites obeyed the instruction they received, and profited by their advantages, they would have been the world's object lesson of health and prosperity. If as a people they had lived according to God's plan, they would have been preserved from the diseases that afflicted other nations. Above any other people they would have possessed physical strength and vigor of intellect. They would have been the mightiest nation on the earth.

The Ministry of Healing, p. 283

Day 3

Prayer for My Church

"*And to the angel of the church in Philadelphia write; These things saith he that is holy, he that is true, he that hath the key of David, he that openeth, and no man man shutteth; and shutteth, and no man openeth; I know thy works: behold, I have set before thee an open door, and no man can shut it: for thou hast a little strength, and hast kept my word, and hast not denied my name.*"

Revelation 3:7, 8

Present truth has always centered on where Jesus is and on what He is doing. At the time of His first advent, present truth pointed to Christ's earthly ministry, which culminated in His death and resurrection. Since then, present truth has revealed Jesus as humanity's High Priest in heaven. In Revelation 3, John sees an open door in heaven, through which the church is invited to pass. This open door leads the way into the heavenly sanctuary, where Jesus applies the merits of His blood shed on the cross to the lives of individual believers. It is the privilege of every Christian to live here, in the heavenly sanctuary, by faith. Some day soon, shortly before Jesus returns, Jesus will end His work of intercession in the heavenly sanctuary, and that door of forgiveness and mercy will be shut. As with Noah's ark, when that door is shut, no man will be able to open it. Pray today that every member of your church will walk through this door of salvation while it is still open.

Sample Prayer

Dear Father in heaven, thank you for providing an open door of salvation through Christ's work of intercession in heaven's temple. Please send Your Holy Spirit's power into the lives of our church family, so that every member may pass through that door by faith into a personal, transforming, saving relationship with Your Son, Jesus Christ.

Reflection

_____

_____

_____

Final Thought

It is those who by faith follow Jesus in the great work of the atonement who receive the benefits of His mediation in their behalf, while those who reject the light which brings to view this work of ministration are not benefited thereby. The Jews who rejected the light given at Christ's first advent, and refused to believe on Him as the Saviour of the world, could not receive pardon through Him. When Jesus at His ascension entered by His own blood into the heavenly sanctuary to shed upon His disciples the blessings of His mediation, the Jews were left in total darkness to continue their useless sacrifices and offerings. The ministration of types and shadows had ceased. That door by which men had formerly found access to God was no longer open. The Jews had refused to seek Him in the only way whereby He could then be found, through the ministration in the sanctuary in heaven. Therefore they found no communion with God. To them the door was shut. They had no knowledge of Christ as the true sacrifice and the only mediator before God; hence they could not receive the benefits of His mediation.

Christ in His Sanctuary, p. 160

Day 4

Prayer for My Community

"Also the sons of the stranger, that join themselves to the Lord, to serve him, and to love the name of the Lord, to be his servants, every one that keepeth the sabbath from polluting it, and taketh hold of my covenant; Even them will I bring to my holy mountain, and make them joyful in my house of prayer: their burnt offerings and their sacrifices shall be accepted upon mine altar; for mine house shall be called a house of prayer for all people."

Isaiah 56:6, 7

Revelation 18 begins with a vision of a mighty angel descending from heaven and covering the earth with great power and light. This symbolic description points to a time just before Jesus returns when God's faithful people will share Bible truth with the world through the unlimited power of the Holy Spirit. The Bible promises that many people who hear this message will recognize it as truth and will take their stand for the seventh-day Sabbath, no matter what the cost may be. Pray today that God will use your church to share this message with your community. Pray today that God will prepare the hearts of those who will hear this message, and that they will accept this message and choose to worship God on His holy day. God promises that as we prayerfully and faithfully do these things, He will bring the strangers through the gates of His temple and into a saving relationship with Him!

Sample Prayer

Dear Jesus, we pray today for the members of our community. We pray that your Holy Spirit will prepare them to hear the truth about You, and about Your seventh-day Sabbath. Please prepare the members of our church to welcome and embrace those that enter Your house of worship.

Reflection

_____

_____

_____

Final Thought

The work of Sabbath reform to be accomplished in the last days is foretold in the prophecy of Isaiah: "Thus saith the Lord, Keep ye judgment, and do justice: for My salvation is near to come, and My righteousness to be revealed. Blessed is the man that doeth this, and the son of man that layeth hold on it; that keepeth the Sabbath from polluting it, and keepeth his hand from doing any evil." "The sons of the stranger, that join themselves to the Lord, to serve Him, and to love the name of the Lord, to be His servants, everyone that keepeth the Sabbath from polluting it, and taketh hold of My covenant; even them will I bring to My holy mountain, and make them joyful in My house of prayer." Isaiah 56:1, 2, 6, 7. These words apply in the Christian age, as shown by the context: "The Lord God which gathereth the outcasts of Israel saith, Yet will I gather others to him, beside those that are gathered unto him." Verse 8. Here is foreshadowed the gathering in of the Gentiles by the gospel. And upon those who then honor the Sabbath, a blessing is pronounced. Thus the obligation of the fourth commandment extends past the crucifixion, resurrection, and ascension of Christ, to the time when His servants should preach to all nations the message of glad tidings.

The Great Controversy, p. 451

The Altar of Burnt Offering

"The next day John seeth Jesus coming unto him, and saith, Behold the Lamb of God, which taketh away the sin of the world."

1 John 1:29

The altar of burnt offering stood inside the courtyard gate. Every animal sacrifice offered on this altar pointed forward to the Messiah and His death on the cross. By his death, Jesus Christ paid the penalty of sin, so that we don't have to. "The wages of sin is death," the Bible states, "but the gift of God is eternal life" (Romans 6:23). The altar of burnt offering represents forgiveness of sin made possible through faith in Jesus Christ.

Day 5

Prayer for Myself

"Let this mind be in you, which was also in Christ Jesus: Who, being in the form of God, thought it not robbery to be equal with God: But made himself of no reputation, and took upon him the form of a servant, and was made in the likeness of men: And being found in fashion as a man, he humbled himself, and became obedient unto death, even the death of the cross."

Philippians 2:5-8

Every Christian is promised that he or she can, through faith, have the mind of Christ. Simply put, this means that Jesus wants to free us from negative, harmful, and destructive patterns of thought. He wants to transform our minds and our hearts so that we value the things He values, love the things He loves, and hate the things He hates. The Bible says in Hebrews 1:9 that God loves righteousness and hates iniquity. When we have the mind of Christ, we also will love what is good and true and hate what is wrong and sinful. When we accept Jesus Christ as our personal Savior, we claim His death on the cross as the payment for our sins. We also accept God's offer to recreate us from the inside out, so that Jesus can live His life of loving obedience to God in and through us. The book of Revelation promises that God will have a people on earth at the end of time that have experienced this transformation in their lives. Revelation 14:12 says, "Here is the patience of the saints: here are they that keep the commandments of God, and the faith of Jesus." Pray today that you will be among this group of people!

Sample Prayer

Dear Father in heaven, You have promised in the Bible that You can give me a new mind and a new heart. You have promised that Jesus can not only forgive my sins, but also cleanse me from all unrighteousness. You have promised that when Jesus returns, You will have people on earth in whom You have worked these miracles. Please fill me with Your Holy Spirit today so that I can be among this group of people.

Reflection

_____

_____

_____

_____

_____

Final Thought

Every one who accepts Christ as his personal Saviour will long for the privilege of serving God. Contemplating what Heaven has done for him, his heart is moved with boundless love and adoring gratitude. He is eager to signalize his gratitude by devoting his abilities to God's service. He longs to show his love for Christ and for his purchased possession. He covets toil, hardship, sacrifice.

Gospel Workers, p. 294

Day 6

Prayer for My Family

"And forgive us our debts, as we forgive our debtors."

Matthew 6:12

When Jesus died on the cross, His sacrifice opened a door for God's grace and forgiveness to be poured out upon the human family. Unfortunately, families today are often missing these two incredibly important things—grace and forgiveness. The devil knows that few wounds hurt as deeply as those caused by the people closest to us, whom we love the most, and, therefore, focuses his attacks on the family. Perhaps your family has unresolved issues of anger or hurt. Maybe lingering grudges, or even unconfessed and unforgiven sin, threaten to destroy your family's peace and love. The Bible counsels us to forgive others, like God has forgiven us. This can often be difficult to do, but God promises to help us extend His grace and forgiveness to those that have hurt us. Pray today that the forgiveness found at the cross of Christ will also be found in your family, and that God will give you the gift of forgiveness toward those that may have hurt you.

Sample Prayer

Dear Father in heaven, the Bible says that all have sinned, and I know that my sins have hurt You deeply. Thank you for promising to forgive me of my sins when I confess and repent them. Please enable me to forgive those that have hurt me, and please unite my family with Your love and grace.

Reflection

_____

_____

_____

_____

_____

Final Thought

When we come to ask mercy and blessing from God we should have a spirit of love and forgiveness in our own hearts. How can we pray, "Forgive us our debts, as we forgive our debtors," and yet indulge an unforgiving spirit? Matthew 6:12. If we expect our own prayers to be heard we must forgive others in the same manner and to the same extent as we hope to be forgiven.

Steps to Christ, p. 97

Day 7

Prayer for My Church

"And what is the exceeding greatness of his power to us-ward who believe, according to the working of his mighty power, Which he wrought in Christ, when he raised him from the dead, and set him at his own right hand in the heavenly places, Far above all principality, and power, and might, and dominion, and every name that is named, not only in this world, but also in that which is to come: And hath put all things under his feet, and gave him to be the head over all things to the church, Which is his body, the fulness of him that filleth all in all."

Ephesians 1:19-23

Because of Jesus Christ's willingness to die on the cross, the Father has now exalted Him "above all principality, and power, and might, and dominion." Jesus uses this power to unite and lead the church, over which He is the Head. The church is called the body of Christ (I Corinthians 12:27), but what does this mean? Consider your body for a moment. Your brain controls all the activities of your body, and many of these functions occur automatically without conscious thought. Imagine what a difficult day you would have if every heartbeat and every breath required a conscious decision on your part! Life would quickly become unbearable, if not completely impossible. In the same way, when the church is fully united to Jesus Christ, He will live His life through every member of the church. His thoughts, His words, and His actions will be demonstrated naturally and almost without conscious effort. Pray today that your church will experience this wonderful reality, and unite under the headship of Jesus.

Sample Prayer

Dear Father in heaven, please unite our church as Christ's body and enable us to follow His lead as our Leader and Head. Please bring Your power, revealed at the cross, into the lives of every church member, so that Christ may be seen in us.

Reflection

_____

_____

_____

Final Thought

The church is built upon Christ as its foundation; it is to obey Christ as its head. It is not to depend upon man, or be controlled by man. Many claim that a position of trust in the church gives them authority to dictate what other men shall believe and what they shall do. This claim God does not sanction. The Saviour declares, "All ye are brethren." All are exposed to temptation, and are liable to error. Upon no finite being can we depend for guidance. The Rock of faith is the living presence of Christ in the church. Upon this the weakest may depend, and those who think themselves the strongest will prove to be the weakest, unless they make Christ their efficiency. "Cursed be the man that trusteth in man, and maketh flesh his arm." The Lord "is the Rock, His work is perfect." "Blessed are all they that put their trust in Him." Jeremiah 17:5; Deuteronomy 32:4; Psalm 2:12.

The Desire of Ages, p. 414

Day 8

Prayer for My Community

"And I, if I be lifted up from the earth, will draw all men unto me."

John 12:32

Jesus promised that all people would be drawn to Him because of the love revealed at His death on the cross. This does not mean, of course, that all people will be saved. But it does mean that God's love is powerful enough to draw anybody to Him—even those who apparently have no interest in spiritual things or in truth. Today we pray for the members of our community, that they all may have every possible opportunity to recognize God's love for them. We also pray that they will respond to God's love, as revealed in Jesus Christ and in the Bible. The Bible reveals that at the end of time many people from unlikely backgrounds will indeed be drawn to God and to truth. In Revelation 18:4, God says, "Come out of [Babylon], my people, that ye be not partakers of her sins, and that ye receive not of her plagues." Pray today that the members of your community will be among those that "come out" of Babylon. Pray today that they will be drawn to Jesus and come into the body of Christ.

Sample Prayer

Dear Father in heaven, the Bible predicts that many people will be drawn to you even at the end of time. We pray today for the members of our community, that this promise will be fulfilled in their lives. We pray that they will accept Jesus Christ's death for them on the cross. We pray that they will accept His offer of new life through baptism. And we pray that they will accept the Bible truths that will help them become committed members of Christ's family here on earth.

Reflection

_____

_____

_____

Final Thought

But the plan of redemption had a yet broader and deeper purpose than the salvation of man. It was not for this alone that Christ came to the earth; it was not merely that the inhabitants of this little world might regard the law of God as it should be regarded; but it was to vindicate the character of God before the universe. To this result of His great sacrifice—its influence upon the intelligences of other worlds, as well as upon man—the Saviour looked forward when just before His crucifixion He said: "Now is the judgment of this world: now shall the prince of this world be cast out. And I, if I be lifted up from the earth, will draw all unto Me." John 12:31, 32. The act of Christ in dying for the salvation of man would not only make heaven accessible to men, but before all the universe it would justify God and His Son in their dealing with the rebellion of Satan. It would establish the perpetuity of the law of God and would reveal the nature and the results of sin.

Patriarchs and Prophets, p. 68

The Laver

"Jesus answered and said unto her, Whosoever drinketh of this water shall thirst again: But whosoever drinketh of the water that I shall give him shall never thirst; but the water that I shall give him shall be in him a well of water springing up into everlasting life."

John 14:13, 14

Between the altar of burnt offering and the tabernacle stood the laver, or washbasin. Before entering the tabernacle, priests were required to wash their hands and feet in the laver's water. This cleansing ritual represented the spiritual cleansing and washing away of sin that is available through faith in Jesus Christ. The priests were the only ones permitted to wash in the laver, but today all who desire a new life in Christ can be baptized. "Know ye not, that so many of us as were baptized into Jesus Christ were baptized into his death? Therefore we are buried with him by baptism into death: that like as Christ was raised up from the dead by the glory of the Father, even so we also should walk in newness of life" (Romans 6:3,4). The laver represents baptism and the new birth experience, which is required to enter heaven.

Day 9

Prayer for Myself

Romans 6:3, 4. "Know ye not, that so many of us as were baptized into Jesus Christ were baptized into his death? Therefore we are buried with him by baptism into death: that like as Christ was raised up from the dead by the glory of the Father, even so we also should walk in newness of life."

Romans 6:3, 4

The Bible says that when Jesus Christ returns at His second coming, "every eye will see Him" (Revelation 1:7). This is a wonderful promise, but also one that should cause us to ask a question: How will this be possible? Here's the problem. When Moses asked God if he could see His face, God responded that no man could see Him and live (Exodus 33:20). Yet Jesus promises that when He returns "in his glory, and all the holy angels with him" (Matthew 25:31), there will be a people that can stand in His presence. How will this be possible? The answer is simple: Those people who stand in Christ's presence must be born again and cleansed from their sins. Pray today that God will forgive you of your sins, wash them away, and enable you to walk in newness of life. Pray that God will give you the desire to forsake these sins and the power to turn from them.

Sample Prayer

Dear Father in heaven, I recognize that baptism is heaven's chosen symbol for the new birth experience that is necessary for entrance into heaven. If I have not been baptized by water immersion, I make the decision today to take this most important step in my life. If I have already been baptized, I ask that You will help me to rise to greater heights in spiritual understanding and to adjust my interests and actions to be in harmony with Your promise of eternity.

Reflection

_____

_____

_____

_____

_____

Final Thought

Those who have taken part in the solemn rite of baptism have pledged themselves to seek for those things which are above, where Christ sitteth on the right hand of God; pledged themselves to labor earnestly for the salvation of sinners. God asks those who take His name, How are you using the powers that have been redeemed by the death of My Son? Are you doing all in your power to rise to a greater height in spiritual understanding? Are you adjusting your interest and actions in harmony with the momentous claims of eternity?"

The Faith I Live By, p. 146

Day 10

Prayer for My Family

"Wives, submit yourselves unto your own husbands, as unto the Lord. For the husband is the head of the wife, even as Christ is the head of the church: and he is the savior of the body. Therefore as the church is subject unto Christ, so let the wives be to their own husbands in every thing. Husbands, love your wives, even as Christ also loved the church, and gave himself for it; That he might sanctify and cleanse it with the washing of water by the word, That he might present it to himself a glorious church, not having spot, or wrinkle, or any such thing; but that it should be holy and without blemish."

Ephesians 5:22-27

The fifth chapter of Ephesians presents a beautiful picture of the relationship that Jesus wants with His church, and also of the peace and love that should characterize every Christian home. God intends that the family be a place where Christian characters are formed, refined, and demonstrated. However, this happens only as the Holy Spirit takes possession of each family member. Is your family suffering from anger, envy, or strife? Pray today that God will fill your home instead with love, humility, and peace. Is your home full of sadness? Pray that God will replace that sadness with joy. God wants to wash away from your family all things that cause division from each other, and from Him. He has promised that He can fill your home with a power that no human eye can see, and effect a life-changing transformation in each member of your family.

Sample Prayer

Dear Father in heaven, Your Son, Jesus Christ, surrendered Himself completely for the salvation of His human family. Please cleanse my family from our sins and from every thing that separates us from You. Fill my family and our home with Christ's Spirit of selfless love, and give us love, humility, peace, and joy.

Reflection

_____

_____

_____

_____

_____

Final Thought

When the Spirit of God takes possession of the heart, it transforms the life. Sinful thoughts are put away, evil deeds are renounced; love, humility, and peace take the place of anger, envy, and strife. Joy takes the place of sadness, and the countenance reflects the light of heaven. The blessing comes when by faith the soul surrenders itself to God. Then that power which no human eye can see creates a new being in the image of God.

The Desire of Ages, p. 173

Day 11

Prayer for My Church

"*You are already clean through the word which I have spoken unto you.*"

John 15:3

Jesus had spent over three years with His disciples, and now He was speaking with them for the very last time before His arrest and crucifixion. What topic would He focus on? Would He again share the prophecies of His death and resurrection? No, these had already been explained numerous times. Would He urge them, one more time, to give up their selfishness and pride? No, these admonitions had also already been repeated. Knowing that He was about to die, Jesus focused on the most important thing He could communicate—the disciples' need of the Holy Spirit to help them abide in Christ. "I am the true vine, and my Father is the husbandman," Jesus said. "Every branch in me that bearers not fruit he taketh away: and every branch that bearers fruit, he purgeth it, that it may bring forth more fruit" (John 15:1, 2). Then Jesus gave this wonderful promise: "Now ye are clean through the word which I have spoken unto you" (John 15:3). Christ's greatest desire for His disciples—and for the church today— is that they be connected with Him through faith in His Word, and that they be cleansed from their sins through this faith in the power of God. Pray today that your local church will seek after this connection with Jesus Christ. Pray that every member in your church will be cleansed from sin "through the word", as Jesus has promised.

Sample Prayer

Dear Father in heaven, the Bible describes the church as the body of Christ. Like any physical body, this spiritual body must remain connected to the Head in order to have life. You have promised that if the church abides by faith in Jesus, you will cleanse it of sin through the power of Your Word. Please make this promise a reality in my local church, today and every day.

Reflection

_____

_____

_____

_____

Final Thought

Wonderful is the work which the Lord designs to accomplish through His church, that His name may be glorified. A picture of this work is given in Ezekiel's vision of the river of healing: "These waters issue out toward the east country, and go down into the desert, and go into the sea: which being brought forth into the sea, the waters shall be healed. And it shall come to pass, that everything that liveth, which moveth, whithersoever the rivers shall come, shall live:... and by the river upon the bank thereof, on this side and on that side, shall grow all trees for meat, whose leaf shall not fade, neither shall the fruit thereof be consumed: it shall bring forth new fruit according to his months, because their waters they issued out of the sanctuary: and the fruit thereof shall be for meat, and the leaf thereof for medicine." Ezekiel 47:8-12.

Acts of the Apostles, p. 13

Day 12

Prayer for My Community

"Know ye not that the unrighteous shall not inherit the kingdom of God? Be
not deceived: neither fornicators, nor idolaters, nor adulterers, nor effemi-
nate, nor abusers of themselves with mankind, Nor thieves, nor covetous, nor
drunkards, nor revilers, nor extortioners, shall inherit the kingdom of God.
And such were some of you: but ye are washed, but ye are sanctified, but ye
are justified in the name of the Lord Jesus, and by the Spirit of our God."

1 Corinthians 6:9-11

The Christians in Corinth lived in an idolatrous, decadent, sensual culture. Before accepting the gospel, many of these church members par-
ticipated in the sinful lifestyles and degrading habits that characterized the
citizens of Corinth. In his letter to the church in Corinth, Paul condemned
the sins so prevalent in that city—sins like fornication, idolatry, adultery,
homosexuality, and thievery. But he also rejoiced that the power of the
gospel had rescued these Christians from their former slavery to sin. "Such
were some of you," wrote Paul, "But ye are washed, but ye are sanctified, but
ye are justified in the name of the Lord Jesus, and by the Spirit of our God."
Pray today that the people in your local community will likewise respond
to the Bible's everlasting gospel of God's forgiveness and transforming love.
Pray that these people will see in you, your family, and your local church,
an accurate picture of Christianity. Pray that they will be washed, sanctified,
and justified through faith in the atoning blood of Jesus Christ.

Sample Prayer

Dear Father in heaven, our local community is filled with many people who do not know You or the power of Your Word. They are trapped in sin, and will perish without the hope of eternal life unless You set them free. Please place Your angels of protection around the people in our community. Please send Your Holy Spirit to convict them of sin, of righteousness, and of judgment. Please transform their lives so that they can be washed from their sins and brought into a life-changing relationship with You.

Reflection

_____

_____

_____

_____

Final Thought

Not by the decisions of courts or councils or legislative assemblies, not by the patronage of worldly great men, is the kingdom of Christ established, but by the implanting of Christ's nature in humanity through the work of the Holy Spirit. "As many as received Him, to them gave He power to become the sons of God, even to them that believe on His name: which were born, not of blood, nor of the will of the flesh, nor of the will of man, but of God." John 1:12, 13. Here is the only power that can work the uplifting of mankind. And the human agency for the accomplishment of this work is the teaching and practicing of the word of God.

The Desire of Ages, p. 509

The Table of Shewbread

"And Jesus said unto them, I am the bread of life: he that cometh to me shall never hunger; and he that believeth on me shall never thirst."

John 6:35

The table of shewbread stood on the north wall of the tabernacle in the Holy Place. It held twelve cakes of bread that were replaced every Sabbath. The bread represents God's presence, as well as His desire to be close to His people, for in ancient times a shared meal symbolized acceptance and unity. The bread represents Jesus, because He identified Himself as "the bread of life." It also points to the Word of God as an indispensable source of spiritual life for every Christian. Daily Bible study and prayer, combined with faith and surrender of self to God, will produce a fruit of righteousness that will not fail to blossom. As the prophet Jeremiah said, "Thy words were found, and I did eat them; and thy word was unto me the joy and rejoicing of mine heart: for I am called by thy name, O Lord God of hosts" (Jeremiah 15:16).

Day 13

Prayer for Myself

"Blessed are the undefiled in the way, who walk in the law of the Lord. Blessed are they that keep his testimonies, and that seek him with the whole heart. They also do no iniquity: they walk in his ways. Thou hast commanded us to keep thy precepts diligently. O that my ways were directed to keep thy statutes! Then shall I not be ashamed, when I have respect unto all thy commandments. I will praise thee with uprightness of heart, when I shall have learned thy righteous judgments."

Psalm 119:1-8

As sinners, we are all naturally attracted to the idea that we can live independently of God—autonomous rulers of our lives, without any law to govern us. This idea was at the core of Satan's first lie to Eve in the Garden of Eden. "[Y]our eyes shall be opened," he said, "and ye shall be as gods, knowing good and evil" (Genesis 3:5). The sad history of sin has proven part of Satan's promise to be true—we certainly know much about evil; however, we definitely are not like God. As for knowing good, most of us can identify with the apostle Paul on a daily basis: "For the good that I would I do not: but the evil which I would not, that I do" (Romans 7:19). There is hope, however. God's law points out clearly the path of peace, safety, and fulfillment for every human being. We don't have the ability to perfectly keep God's law on our own, but Jesus promises to give us His power to obey God and to live a life in harmony with the principles of His Word. Pray today that you will desire to walk in the path of God's law. Pray that you will experience joy and peace as you do this every day.

Sample Prayer

Dear Father in heaven, the Bible promises blessings when we live in harmony with the principles of Your law. As a sinner, I naturally desire to live life my own way, which is frequently not according to Your will or Your Word. Please create in me a desire to accept Your will for my life, and to give You my loving obedience. Please help me to find joy and peace in the Bible and in Your law.

Reflection

_____

_____

_____

_____

_____

Final Thought

God, the great governor of the universe, has put everything under law. The tiny flower and the towering oak, the grain of sand and the mighty ocean, sunshine and shower, wind and rain, all obey nature's laws. But man has been placed under a higher law. He has been given an intellect to see, and a conscience to feel, the powerful claims of God's great moral law, the expression of what He desires His children to be.

Our High Calling, p. 137

Day 14

Prayer for My Family

"*Therefore shall ye lay upon these my words in your heart and in your soul, and bind them for a sign upon your hand, that they may be as frontlets between your eyes. And ye shall teach them your children, speaking of them when thou sittest in thine house, and when thou walkest by the way, when thou liest down, and when thou risest up. And thou shalt write them upon the door posts of thine house, and upon thy gates: That your days may be multiplied, and the days of your children, in the land which the Lord share unto your fathers to give them, as the days of heaven upon the earth.*"

Deuteronomy 11:18-21

God instructed the ancient Israelites to surround their homes and their families with the Word of God. Store them "in your heart and your soul," He told them, "and bind them for a sign upon your hand, that they may be as frontlets between your eyes." In other words, everything they thought and everything they did was to be in harmony with the principles of the Word of God. They were also to take every opportunity possible to teach their children about God and His Word. No matter where they were or what they were doing, the instructions found in God's Word was to be their guide. The imagery of God's Word being written on the "posts of thine house, and upon thy gates" was a graphic depiction of the strength and security that God's Word provides to all who accept it as the rule of their lives. Pray today that your family will allow God's Word to determine all that happens in your home.

Sample Prayer

Dear Father in heaven, thank you for calling my family to be among those that overcome this world. I realize that we can only overcome through the blood of the Lamb and the word of our testimony and by allowing the Bible to determine all that happens in our home. Please write the principles of Your word on our minds and hearts, and help me to exemplify and teach these principles to the other members of my family.

Reflection

_____

_____

_____

_____

_____

Final Thought

God has given His people positive instruction, and has laid upon them positive restrictions, that they may obtain a perfect experience in His service, and be qualified to stand before the heavenly universe and before the fallen world as overcomers. They are to overcome by the blood of the Lamb and the word of their testimony. Those who fall short of making the preparation essential will be numbered with the unthankful and the unholy.

To Be Like Jesus, p. 66

Day 15

Prayer for My Church

Let the word of Christ dwell in you richly in all wisdom; teaching and admonishing one another in psalms and hymns and spiritual songs, singing with grace in your hearts to the Lord. And whatsoever ye do in word or deed, do all in the name of the Lord Jesus, giving thanks to God and the Father by him."

Colossians 3:16, 17

Jesus told His disciples that the words He spoke to them, if accepted and acted upon by faith, would cleanse and purify them from sin. To fulfill its purpose in the world, the church must also be washed through obedience to the Word of God. Its purpose cannot be fulfilled by adopting contemporary worship styles that appeal to the carnal heart. Its purpose cannot be fulfilled by aligning with politically correct and socially acceptable agendas that have nothing to do with the everlasting gospel and the Three Angels' Messages. Its purpose cannot be fulfilled by hiding or minimizing those doctrines and prophecies that set us apart from the world. Its purpose can only be fulfilled when we allow the Bible to have complete authority, from the local church level to the world church level. Pray today that your local church will sense its need to be washed by the Word of God, and follow its authority in every aspect of its worship, leadership structure, evangelism, and church life.

Sample Prayer

Dear Father in heaven, I pray today for my local church family. I pray that all of us as a church family will feel our need to be washed and cleansed of sin. I pray that we will choose to follow the Bible's authority in our own lives, in our families, and in our local church. We need the Word of God to dwell richly within us, and we thank you for making this promise a reality in our lives as we respond in faith.

Reflection

_____

_____

_____

Final Thought

 You will always have erring ones among you, and here is where you can show a Christian character. Do not push them away from you, but if you have light seek to let it shine upon them, and in this way you can help them toward heaven. Every soul that has the spirit of Christ will work the works of Christ. And if any see one wandering away from Christ, he will feel as Christ did about the lost sheep. There were ninety and nine in the fold, but He went out after the one that had strayed away. This is the spirit we should manifest. As children of God we should walk in the light, and as we follow in the light we shall lighten the path for others. Let us cultivate gratitude to God and then we shall not get our eyes upon little difficulties. And although our brethren and sisters may err, shall we err? We have faults, as well as they, and we want compassion, as well as they; we should have compassion for one another.

In High Places, p. 289

Day 16

Prayer for My Community

"Cast thy bread upon the waters: for thou shalt find it after many days. Give a portion to seven, and also to eight; for thou knowest not what evil shall be upon the earth."

Ecclesiastes 11:1, 2

The Bible uses many symbols for the Word of God, and one of those symbols is bread. For example, when Satan tempted Jesus in the wilderness to turn stones into bread, Jesus responded by saying, "Man shall not live by bread alone, but by every word that proceeds from the mouth of God." Another symbol in the Bible is water, which, as used in prophecy, represents a population of people. Our verse today, then, encourages us to share Bible truth with the people around us and promises that these efforts will bring results. The world today is hungry. Yes, in many cases this hunger is very physical in nature, but an even greater famine of spiritual hunger plagues all nations. Many people are looking for truth but don't know where to find it. Pray today that the people in your community will find the truth and accept the everlasting gospel and the Three Angels' Messages. Pray that they will be set free from error and from sin through the power of God's Word.

Sample Prayer

Dear Father in heaven, I pray today for the people in my community, that they will hear and accept the everlasting gospel and the Three Angels' Messages. I pray that they will be set free from error and from sin. Please break the spell of Satan's deceptions that may be blinding their minds and their hearts. Please do this miraculous work in such a way that others will recognize it and be led to surrender their lives to you as well.

Reflection

_____

_____

_____

Final Thought

The teaching of the Bible has a vital bearing upon man's prosperity in all the relations of this life. It unfolds the principles that are the cornerstone of a nation's prosperity—principles with which is bound up the well being of society, and which are the safeguard of the family—principles without which no man can attain usefulness, happiness, and honor in this life, or can hope to secure the future, immortal life. There is no position in life, no phase of human experience, for which the teaching of the Bible is not an essential preparation. Studied and obeyed, the Word of God would give to the world men of stronger and more active intellect than will the closest application to all the subjects that human philosophy embraces. It would give men of strength and solidity of character, of keen perception and sound judgment—men who would be an honor to God and a blessing to the world.

The Remnant Church, p. 115

The Altar of Incense

"Seeing then that we have a great high priest, that is passed into the heavens, Jesus the Son of God, let us hold fast our profession. For we have not a high priest which cannot be touched with the feeling of our infirmities; but was in all points tempted like as we are, yet without sin. Let us therefore come boldly unto the throne of grace, that we may obtain mercy, and find grace to help in time of need."

Hebrews 4:14-16

The altar of incense sat directly in front of the tabernacle's second curtain separating the Holy Place from the Most Holy Place. It was the piece of furniture in the Holy Place that sat closest to the Ark of the Covenant and the presence of God. Every day the priests offered incense on this altar; their work here represented the intercession of Jesus Christ in heaven's sanctuary. Hebrews 7:25 assures us that "Jesus ever liveth to make intercession for [us]," and the book of Revelation pictures Him standing at the altar of incense as He presents our prayers to the Father. "And another angel came and stood at the altar, having a golden censer; and there was given unto him much incense, that he should offer it with the prayers of all saints upon the golden altar which was before the throne" (Revelation 8:3). The altar of incense represents Christ's intercession in heaven as He listens to our prayers and presents them to the Father.

Day 17

Prayer for Myself

"And Jacob was left alone; and there wrestled a man with him until the breaking of the day. And when he saw that he prevailed not against him, he touched the hollow of his thigh; and the hollow of Jacob's thigh was out of joint, as he wrestled with him. And he said, Let me go, for the day breaketh. And he said, I will not let thee go, except thou bless me. And he said unto him, What is thy name? And he said, Jacob. And he said, Thy name shall be called no more Jacob, but Israel: for as a prince hast thou power with God and with men, and hast prevailed."

Genesis 32:24-28

Before Jacob's night of wrestling with the angel, his experience had been characterized by selfishness, pride, and deception. Multiple damaged relationships marked the footsteps of this self-seeking patriarch. However, Jacob's turning point came when he realized that his only hope of salvation was through complete dependence on God. The blessing of forgiveness and cleansing came, and was marked by a new name—Israel—which means "God prevails." That night of trial represents the experience that every Christian must pass through if he or she will be saved. It also points forward to the time of trouble. In that time, every known sin will need to have been confessed and forsaken. And as with Jacob, the promise is given to us today that a new name and character will be the reward of earnest seeking after God. Pray today that you will seek after Christ and His righteousness with the same fervor and commitment that Jacob did.

Sample Prayer

Dear Father in heaven, thank you for the assurance that when we seek for You with our whole heart, You will be found. I recognize my need of a new character. Like Jacob, I am selfish, proud, and often speak and act in a way that denies my claim to be a Christian. Please forgive me of my sins and cleanse me from all unrighteousness as You have promised in 1 John 1:9. Please give me a new character, as you did for Jacob.

Reflection

_____

_____

_____

Final Thought

Jacob's night of anguish, when he wrestled in prayer for deliverance from the hand of Esau (Genesis 32:24-30), represents the experience of God's people in the time of trouble. ...Had not Jacob previously repented of his sin in obtaining the birthright by fraud, God would not have heard his prayer and mercifully preserved his life. So, in the time of trouble, if the people of God had unconfessed sins to appear before them while tortured with fear and anguish, they would be overwhelmed; despair would cut off their faith, and they could not have confidence to plead with God for deliverance. But while they have a deep sense of their unworthiness, they have no concealed wrongs to reveal. Their sins have gone beforehand to judgment and have been blotted out, and they cannot bring them to remembrance.

The Great Controversy, pp. 616, 620

Day 18

Prayer for My Family

"Behold, I will send you Elijah the prophet before the coming of the great and dreadful day of the Lord: And he shall turn the heart of the fathers to the children, and the heart of the children to their fathers, lest I come and smite the earth with a curse."

Malachi 4:5, 6

The final verses of the Old Testament present a magnificent promise: before the Lord comes, He will accomplish a work of restoration within many families. As the prophet Malachi says with great hope, "He shall turn the heart of the fathers to the children, and the heart of the children to their fathers." Are the members of your family separated by conflict or deep differences of opinion? Do you have loved ones that have wandered far from God and from Bible truth? God promises that He will do all in heaven's power to restore your family to each other, and to Him, before the second coming of Jesus Christ. Pray today that Malachi's promise will be fulfilled in your family. Pray that God will reveal His power within your family. Pray that this miracle will be a blessing and encouragement to someone else.

Sample Prayer

Dear Father in heaven, today I claim your promise in Malachi 4:5-6, that you will turn the heart of the fathers to the children, and the heart of the children to their fathers. You know that pain and division exist in my family. You know the doubt and lack of belief that some of my family members struggle with. Please reveal your power of reconciliation and healing in my family, and prepare all of us for your soon return.

Reflection

_____

_____

_____

_____

Final Thought

Parents may understand that as they follow God's directions in the training of their children, they will receive help from on high. They receive much benefit; for as they teach, they learn. Their children will achieve victories through the knowledge that they have acquired in keeping the way of the Lord. They are enabled to overcome natural and hereditary tendencies to evil. ...Parents, are you working with unflagging energy in behalf of your children? The God of heaven marks your solicitude, your earnest work, your constant watchfulness. He hears your prayers. With patience and tenderness train your children for the Lord. All heaven is interested in your work.... God will unite with you, crowning your efforts with success.

The Adventist Home, p. 205

Day 19

Prayer for My Church

"Is any among you afflicted? Let him pray. Is any merry? Let him sing psalms. Is any sick among you? Let him call for the elders of the church; and let them pray over him, anointing him with oil in the name of the Lord: And the prayer of faith shall save the sick, and the Lord shall raise him up; and if he have committed sins, they shall be forgiven him. Confess your faults one to another, and pray one for another, that ye may be healed. The effectual fervent prayer of a righteous man availeth much."

James 5:13-16

The Bible calls the church the body of Christ. Like the parts of a healthy body work in harmony with each other, so should the members within the local church. Of course, this is not always the case, and far too many church families are plagued by gossip, distrust, and evil surmising. Praying for each other is effective medicine for these deadly diseases. James encouraged Christians to "confess your faults one to another, and pray one for another, that ye may be healed." God's answer may at times include miracles of physical healing, but the promise also refers to spiritual healing, seen through restored relationships and rebuilt trust. Pray today that the Holy Spirit will prompt members of your local church to confess to each other those wrongs and faults that need to be forgiven. Pray that each member and each family of your church will pray for each other, and that God will unleash His healing power in your church.

Sample Prayer

Dear Father in heaven, You have promised that "the prayer of faith shall save the sick, and the Lord shall raise him up." You know that our local church family needs this healing power. You know the physical ailments that afflict many of the members of our church. Please heal their bodies, if it will bring you glory. You also know the spiritual and relational challenges that threaten to divide and destroy our church. Please convict each member in this church body of the confession and forgiveness that is needed to restore truth, trust, and love in our congregation.

Reflection

_____

_____

_____

_____

_____

Final Thought

Let us learn to pray intelligently, expressing our requests with clearness and precision. Let us put away the listless, sluggish habit into which we have fallen, and pray as though we meant it. "The effectual fervent prayer of a righteous man availeth much." [James 5:16.] Faith takes a firm hold of the promises of God, and urges her petitions with fervor; but when the life of the soul stagnates, the outward devotions become formal and powerless.

Gospel Workers, p. 426

Day 20

Prayer for My Community

"I exhort therefore that, first of all, supplications, prayers, intercessions, and giving of thanks, be made for all men; For kings, and for all that are in authority; that we may lead a quiet and peaceable life in all godliness and honesty. For this is good and acceptable in the sight of God our Saviour; Who will have all men to be saved, and to come unto the knowledge of the truth."

1 Timothy 2:1-4

The Bible urges Christians to pray for all people, especially "kings, and for all that are in authority." These prayers of intercession are important for several reasons. First, spiritual deception continues to increase, and the Bible warns that many people will perish "because they received not the love of the truth, that they might be saved" (2 Thessalonians 2:10). Pray today that the members of your community will learn—and fall in love with—Bible truth. Second, the world is under the control of a mighty fallen angel, and Scripture refers to his kingdom as spiritual Babylon—a place controlled by "the merchants of the earth" (Revelation 18:11). Pray today that the members of your community will not be ensnared by the material things of this world, and that they will instead be captivated by the love of God. Finally, Bible prophecy reveals that laws will eventually be passed around the world restricting freedom of conscience and freedom of worship. Pray today that the leaders in your community and the rulers in your country will uphold the principles of God's law.

Sample Prayer

Dear Father in heaven, thank you for the people in my community. You know that many of them are honest seekers after truth, but that many of them simply don't know where to find that truth. Please work in their lives so that they may learn about You and about Bible truth. Please use me, my family, and my church to bring them to a knowledge of Bible prophecy and the law of God, so that they may stand with Your people in earth's final events.

Reflection

_____

_____

_____

Final Thought

In dealing with unreasonable and wicked men, those who believe the truth are to be careful not to bring themselves down to the same level, where they will use the same Satanic weapons that their enemies use, by giving loose rein to strong personal feelings, and arousing against themselves and against the work the Lord has given them to do, passion and bitter enmity. Keep Jesus uplifted. We are laborers together with God. We are provided with spiritual weapons, mighty to the pulling down of the strongholds of the enemy. We must in no case misrepresent our faith by weaving unChristlike attributes into the work. We must exalt the law of God, as binding us up with Jesus Christ and all who love Him and keep His commandments. We are also to reveal a love for the souls for whom Christ has died. Our faith is to be demonstrated as a power of which Christ is the Author. And the Bible, His word, is to make us wise unto salvation.

Manuscript 46, 1898, pp. 7-11

The Candlestick

"Then spake Jesus again unto them, saying, I am the light of the world: he that followeth me shall not walk in darkness, but shall have the light of life."

John 8:12

The candlestick stood against the south wall of the holy place. Its seven lamp stands were fed by a continuous supply of oil, and its light pushed back the darkness that otherwise would have enveloped the holy place. The candlestick represents Jesus, Who said, "I am the light of the world." But it also represents Jesus living His life through His people—the church. Just as the flames of the candlestick were kept alive by the supply of oil, Christians can reflect the character of Jesus only as they are filled with the Holy Spirit. The candlestick is a powerful symbol of the effect that the church, a single family, and individual Christians can have in the lives of the people around them.

Day 21

Prayer for Myself

"I counsel thee to buy of me gold tried in the fire, that thou mayest be rich; and white raiment, that thou mayest be clothed, and that the shame of thy nakedness do not appear; and anoint thine eyes with eye salve, that thou mayest see."

Revelation 3:18

The letter to the Laodicean church reveals a shocking reality—God's professed people today are "wretched, miserable, poor, blind, and naked" (Revelation 3:17). We are wretched because we know what is right, but continue living as slaves of sin (Romans 7:25). We are miserable because we are living more for this world than for heaven (1 Corinthians 15:19). We are poor because we have slighted God's mercy in a time of judgment (Romans 2:4). We are blind because we have ignored the light of Bible prophecy (2 Peter 1:19). And we are naked because we have rejected Christ's robe of righteousness (Revelation 19:8), preferring instead an imitation righteousness based on human standards. This straight testimony can be hard to hear, and even more difficult to accept! But Jesus reveals this truth because He loves His people. Pray today that you will buy Christ's gold tried in the fire and live a life of faith that works by love. Pray that you will accept Christ's white raiment and experience His power over your sin and righteousness. Pray that you will be anointed with the divine eye salve and be able to see yourself and others as Jesus does.

Sample Prayer

Dear Father in heaven, You know that I desire to serve You with an undivided heart. However, I am weak and so often distrust You and dishonor You in my words and my actions. Thank you for loving me in spite of my spiritual weakness. Please give me today faith, hope, and love straight from heaven's throne, and wrap me in Christ's righteousness. Please give me eye salve that I can see myself and others the way you do.

Reflection

_____

_____

_____

_____

_____

Final Thought

The gold that Jesus would have us buy of Him is gold tried in the fire; it is the gold of faith and love, that has no defiling substance mingled with it. The white raiment is the righteousness of Christ, the wedding garment which Christ alone can give. The eyesalve is the true spiritual discernment that is so wanting among us, for spiritual things must be spiritually discerned.

The Review and Herald, April 1, 1890

Day 22

Prayer for My Family

"Ye are the light of the world. A city that is set on a hill cannot be hid. Neither do men light a candle, and put it under a bushel, but on a candlestick; and it giveth light unto all that are in the house. Let your light so shine before men, that they may see your good works, and glorify your Father which is in heaven."

Matthew 4:15-16

One of the most powerful witnesses for truth is a well-ordered Christian family powered by the love of the Holy Spirit. Such a family is like a city set on a hill, reflecting the light of truth on all with whom they interact. God created the first family in the Garden of Eden, and He intended that this family would "be fruitful, and multiply, and replenish the earth, and subdue it" (Genesis 1:28). Sin has taken a mighty toll on the family, and the family unit is under heavy attack in the world today. Satan loves nothing more than to destroy the peace, love, and unity of Christian homes. However, the Bible promises that God will place His angels of protection around all who ask for help and trust in His power. By God's grace, families can still play an important role in the final proclamation of the gospel to all the world. Pray today that your family will be like a light set on a hill. Pray that the people with whom your family interacts will see your good works, and glorify your Father which is in heaven.

Sample Prayer

Dear Father in heaven, please make my family a light by which others in my church and community may see you more clearly. Please protect my family from the attacks of the enemy. Grant us heavenly wisdom, courage, and strength, so that Your kingdom may be fruitful and multiply through our witness. Please use my family in the final proclamation of the gospel.

Reflection

_____

_____

_____

_____

_____

Final Thought

God desires that heaven's plan shall be carried out, and heaven's divine order and harmony prevail, in every family, in every church, in every institution. Did this love leaven society, we should see the outworking of noble principles in Christian refinement and courtesy and in Christian charity toward the purchase of the blood of Christ. Spiritual transformation would be seen in all our families, in our institutions, in our churches. When this transformation takes place, these agencies will become instrumentalities by which God will impart heaven's light to the world and thus, through divine discipline and training, fit men and women for the society of heaven.

The Adventist Home, p. 535

Day 23

Prayer for My Church

"Go ye therefore, and teach all nations, baptizing them in the name of the Father, and of the Son, and of the Holy Ghost: Teaching them to observe all tings whatsoever I have commanded you: and lo, I am with you alway, even unto the end of the world. Amen."

Matthew 28:19, 20

The church exists for one reason, and one reason alone: It is God's appointed agency to save people from the power of sin. It accomplishes this mission through service, through preaching of the gospel, and through teaching of the truth. To the degree that the church becomes sidetracked from this one purpose, it fails to glorify God and falls short of its appointed mission. When the church begins acting like a social club, a base for political activism, or a platform for the latest social movement, it loses its purpose and becomes destined to conform with the very world that it is called to change. Pray today that your local church will maintain, or regain if necessary, its divinely given mission and purpose. Pray that it will reflect to the world God's fullness and His sufficiency. Pray that your church, and each member in it, will glorify God in all that is said and done.

Sample Prayer

Dear Father in heaven, thank you for creating and organizing my local church family. You have purposed that it will be a heaven-appointed agency for the salvation of souls in our community. Please enable us to stay focused on our mission of uplifting Jesus, sharing present truth, and serving the people around us. Please fill this church with the power of the Holy Spirit so that You will be glorified in all that is said and done.

Reflection

_____

_____

_____

_____

_____

Final Thought

The church is God's appointed agency for the salvation of men. It was organized for service, and its mission is to carry the gospel to the world. From the beginning it has been God's plan that through His church shall be reflected to the world His fullness and His sufficiency. The members of the church, those whom He has called out of darkness into His marvelous light, are to show forth His glory. The church is the repository of the riches of the grace of Christ; and through the church will eventually be made manifest, even to "the principalities and powers in heavenly places," the final and full display of the love of God. Ephesians 3:10.

Acts of the Apostles, p. 9

Day 24

Prayer for My Community

"But rise, and stand upon thy feet: for I have appeared unto thee for this purpose, to make thee a minister and a witness both of these things which thou hast seen, and of those things in the which I will appear unto thee; Delivering thee from the people, and from the Gentiles, unto whom now I send thee, To open their eyes, and to turn them from darkness to light, and from the power of Satan unto God, that they may receive forgiveness of sins, and inheritance among them which are sanctified by faith that is in me."

Acts 26:16-18

The Bible says, "All have sinned, and fallen short of the glory of God" (Romans 3:23). Human beings are Satan's lawful captives, and of ourselves we have no chance of overcoming sin or obtaining eternal life. However, even though "the wages of sin is death, the gift of God is eternal life through Jesus Christ our Lord" (Romans 6:23). The process of salvation is explained in Acts 26:16-18. First, our eyes must be opened to the truth of our helpless condition. Second, we must choose to turn from darkness to light; as we do this, God frees us from Satan's power. Third, when we confess our sins, God promises to "forgive us our sins, and to cleanse us from all unrighteousness" (1 John 1:9). Finally, this miraculous transformation of character leads to an eternal inheritance. Pray today that the members of your local community will experience every step in God's plan of salvation. Pray that they will turn from the power of Satan to the power of God.

Sample Prayer

Dear Father in heaven, our community is filled with people who do not know You or Your power. They are trapped by Satan's lies and by destructive habits that continually drag them further and further from truth and from a relationship with You. Please work in the lives of every person in our community, that they may experience the power of God's transforming love. Please rescue them from Satan's power and bring them into Your truth.

Reflection

_____

_____

_____

_____

_____

Final Thought

Fallen man is Satan's lawful captive. The mission of Jesus Christ was to rescue him from his power. Man is naturally inclined to follow Satan's suggestions, and he cannot of himself successfully resist so terrible a foe, unless Christ, the mighty conqueror, dwells in him, guiding his desires, and giving him strength. God alone can limit the power of Satan. He is going to and fro in the earth, and walking up and down in it. He is not off his watch for a single moment, through fear of losing an opportunity to destroy souls. It is important that God's people understand this, that they may escape his snares.

Messages to Young People, p. 51

The Ark of the Covenant

"Then said I, Lo, I come: in the volume of the book it is written of me, I delight to do thy will, O my God: yea, thy law is within my heart."

Psalm 40:7, 8

The ark of the covenant was the only piece of furniture in the Most Holy Place. It consisted of a gold-covered wooden box with a golden lid, on top of which were two gold cherubim. One of the items found in the box was the Ten Commandments, a replica of God's law in heaven. The golden lid contained the mercy seat, on which atoning blood was sprinkled each year on the Day of Atonement. At the end of this day, the children of Israel were symbolically "clean from all [their] sins before the Lord" (Leviticus 16:30). This solemn day pointed forward in time to the final cleansing of God's people through Christ's work in the heavenly sanctuary. At the end of this cleansing work, Jesus Christ will have a people who are prepared to meet Him, because they will be cleansed from sin: "That he might present it to himself a glorious church, not having spot, or wrinkle, or any such thing; but that it should be holy and without blemish" (Ephesians 5:27). Jesus delighted to do the Father's will, and for those who love Him, God promises to "put my laws into their mind, and write them in their hearts" (Hebrews 8:10). The ark of the covenant represents the union of divinity and humanity that is possible through faith in God's promises.

Day 25

Prayer for Myself

"The law of the Lord is perfect, converting the soul: the testimony of the Lord is sure, making wise the simple. The statutes of the Lord are right, rejoicing the heart: the commandment of the Lord is pure, enlightening the eyes. The fear of the Lord is clean, enduring for ever: the judgments of the Lord are true and righteous altogether. More to be desired are they than gold, yea, than much fine gold: sweeter also than honey and the honeycomb. Moreover by them is thy servant warned: and in keeping of them there is great reward. Who can understand his errors? Cleanse thou me from secret faults. Keep back thy servant also from presumptuous sins; let them not have dominion over me: then shall I be upright, and I shall be innocent from the great transgression."

Psalm 19:7-13

In the Sermon on the Mount, Jesus explained the principles of the Ten Commandments, explaining that true obedience to God's law is not based on outward actions, but on our hidden thoughts and motives. Cleansing from sin, therefore, requires that our minds and hearts be controlled by the Holy Spirit. Only through this connection with divine power can we recognize, much less overcome, our sinful habits, tendencies, and weaknesses. Pray today that the Holy Spirit will take control of your thoughts, motives, and actions. Pray that His divine power will help you recognize both the secret and obvious things in your life that would keep you separated from Jesus and keep you a captive to sin.

Sample Prayer

Dear Father in heaven, the deceptive power of sin is great. Without Your help, I am in constant danger of ignoring my sins, and even of failing to recognize them. Please fill me with Your Holy Spirit today, and take control of my thoughts, motives, and actions. Please help me recognize the secret and obvious sins in my life that keep me separated from a closer walk with Jesus Christ.

Reflection

_____

_____

_____

_____

_____

Final Thought

Presumption is Satan's counterfeit of faith. Faith claims God's promises, and brings forth fruit in obedience. Presumption also claims the promises, but uses them as Satan did, to excuse transgression. Faith would have led our first parents to trust the love of God, and to obey His commands. Presumption led them to transgress His law, believing that His great love would save them from the consequence of their sin. It is not faith that claims the favor of Heaven without complying with the conditions on which mercy is to be granted. Genuine faith has its foundation in the promises and provisions of the Scriptures."

The Desire of Ages, p. 126

Day 26

Prayer for My Family

"Finally, brethren, whatsoever things are true, whatsoever things are honest, whatsoever things are just, whatsoever things are pure, whatsoever things are lovely, whatsoever things are of good report; if there be any virtue, and if there be any praise, think on these things."

Philippians 4:8

Philippians 4:8 clearly describes what a Christian home guarded by the principles of God's law will look like. Only those things that are true and honest will find a place within that home, which should prompt some introspection. What kind of reading material, movies, and other forms of media and entertainment are in my home? Are they true and honest? What kinds of conversations find their way into our living room or dining room? The Bible's filter will also exclude from the Christian family those things that are not pure, loving, or of a good report. Gossip, competition, and envy are all among humanity's most-loved past times, but they should have no part in a Christian home. Instead, encourage the members of your family to think and speak the best of others. Even in this sinful world, God has preserved numerous things of virtue that are worthy of praise. Pray today that your family and your home will be a place guarded by the principles of righteousness found in God's law. Your home will be a happier and more peaceful place when the Bible determines all that is done in your home!

Sample Prayer

Dear Father in heaven, today I pray for my home, and for every member of my family. Please create within us a love for things that are true, honest, pure, lovely, and of good report. Please create within us a distaste and a hatred for all things sinful, harmful, and destructive. May the Bible be the standard of conduct and speech within our home, and may we all learn to love and cherish Your law of love more and more each day.

Reflection

_____

_____

_____

Final Thought

Yet we have a work to do to resist temptation. Those who would not fall a prey to Satan's devices must guard well the avenues of the soul; they must avoid reading, seeing, or hearing that which will suggest impure thoughts. The mind should not be left to wander at random upon every subject that the adversary of souls may suggest. "Girding up the loins of your mind," says the apostle Peter, "Be sober, ...not fashioning yourselves according to your former lusts in...your ignorance: but like as He which called you is holy, be ye yourselves also holy in all manner of living." 1 Peter 1:13-15, R.V. ...This will require earnest prayer and unceasing watchfulness. We must be aided by the abiding influence of the Holy Spirit, which will attract the mind upward, and habituate it to dwell on pure and holy things. And we must give diligent study to the word of God.

Patriarchs and Prophets, p. 460

Day 27

Prayer for My Church

"These things write I unto thee, hoping to come unto thee shortly: But if I tarry long, that thou mayest know how thou oughtest to behave in the house of God, which is the church of the living God, the pillar and ground of the truth."

1 Timothy 3:14, 15

The Bible doesn't have much good to say about this world. In fact, it states that "the whole world lieth in wickedness" (1 John 5:19). However, the Bible is clear that God has established one thing in this sinful world that is meant to represent Him and the truth. That thing is the church—"the pillar and ground of the truth." Unfortunately, the members of God's church have frequently chosen to compromise with the world instead of remaining faithful to the God and His Word. They have often adopted the world's customs and values rather than treasure and share the habits and values of heaven. But there have always been a few who choose to remain faithful to God and to His law. The Bible promises that even at the end of time, there will be a faithful remnant who follow Jesus wherever He goes, and as a result "are without fault before the throne of God" (Revelation 14:5). Pray today that your local church will be among this group of faithful people. Pray that you and every other member of your church family will choose to follow Jesus wherever He goes. Pray that your church will be a pillar and ground of the truth in your community.

Sample Prayer

Dear Father in heaven, You have established my local church to be the pillar and ground of truth in its community. Please encourage and strengthen each member of my church today, and enable by Your grace to follow Jesus wherever He goes. Please create within us a love for the truth and for Your law, and help this love to be evident to the people around us.

Reflection

_____

_____

_____

_____

Final Thought

The church is God's fortress, His city of refuge, which He holds in a revolted world. Any betrayal of the church is treachery to Him who has bought mankind with the blood of His only-begotten Son. From the beginning, faithful souls have constituted the church on earth. In every age the Lord has had His watchmen, who have borne a faithful testimony to the generation in which they lived. These sentinels gave the message of warning; and when they were called to lay off their armor, others took up the work. God brought these witnesses into covenant relation with Himself, uniting the church on earth with the church in heaven. He has sent forth His angels to minister to His church, and the gates of hell have not been able to prevail against His people.

Acts of the Apostles, p. 11

Day 28

Prayer for My Community

> *"And then shall that Wicked be revealed, whom the Lord shall consume with the spirit of his mouth, and shall destroy with the brightness of his coming: Even him, whose coming is after the working of Satan will all power and signs and lying wonders, And with all deceivableness of unrighteousness in them that perish; because they received not the love of the truth, that they might be saved. And for this cause God shall send them strong delusion, that they should believe a lie: That they all might be damned who believed not the truth, but had pleasure in unrighteousness."*
>
> 2 Thessalonians 2:8-12

Spiritual and sensory deceptions will flood this world at the end of time. Sadly, most people will make decisions for eternity based on lies, deceptions, and blind faith in what they feel to be true. Satan's deceptions are aimed at all classes of people. Carnal sins capture many, while human philosophy and "science falsely so called" (1 Timothy 6:20) ensnare others. The apostle Paul warned that people will not be lost because they believed a lie, but rather because they "received not the love of the truth, that they might be saved." Human nature prefers those lies and deceptions that make us believe we are okay just as we are, without the need of a Savior. This is why we must turn to God and ask Him to help us learn to love the truth. Pray today that the people in your community will see through the devil's many deceptions. Pray that they will learn to love the truth and be saved.

Sample Prayer

Dear Father in heaven, our community is filled with people that do not know the truth. Some of them are looking for truth but don't know where to find it. Others don't seem to care at all, but prefer to live based on their feelings and inclinations. Please work powerfully for all of these people today. Please help them to see through the devil's deceptions, and bring them to a love of the truth through the power of Your Holy Spirit.

Reflection

_____

_____

_____

Final Thought

The prince of darkness, who has so long bent the powers of his mastermind to the work of deception, skillfully adapts his temptations to men of all classes and conditions. To persons of culture and refinement he presents spiritualism in its more refined and intellectual aspects, and thus succeeds in drawing many into his snare. The wisdom which spiritualism imparts is that described by the apostle James, which "descendeth not from above, but is earthly, sensual, devilish." James 3:15. This, however, the great deceiver conceals when concealment will best suit his purpose. He who could appear clothed with the brightness of the heavenly seraphs before Christ in the wilderness of temptation, comes to men in the most attractive manner as an angel of light. He appeals to the reason by the presentation of elevating themes; he delights the fancy with enrapturing scenes; and he enlists the affections by his eloquent portrayals of love and charity. He excites the imagination to lofty flights, leading men to take so great pride in their own wisdom that in their hearts they despise the Eternal One.

The Great Controversy, p. 553

Concluding Prayers

Day 29

Prayer for a Finished People

"And he gave some, apostles; and some, prophets; and some, evangelists; and some, pastors and teachers; For the perfecting of the saints for the work of the ministry, for the edifying of the body of Christ: Till we all come in the unity of the faith, and of the knowledge of the Son of God, unto a perfect man, unto the measure of the stature of the fullness of Christ: That we henceforth be no more children, tossed to and fro, and carried about with every wind of doctrine, by the sleight of men, and cunning craftiness, whereby they lie in wait to deceive; But speaking the truth in love, may grow up into him in all things, which is the head, even Christ."

Ephesians 4:11-15

The book of Revelation speaks about a group of people at the end of time that remain faithful to God and the Bible in spite of intense opposition from the rest of the world. This group is described in Revelation 14:12 as keeping "the commandments of God, and the faith of Jesus." How did they achieve this unity with each other and with Jesus? Ephesians 4 gives us the answer: They have "grow[n] up into him in all things, which is the head, even Christ" (verse 15). In other words, they have spent time with Jesus, and He has transformed them into His image so that they reflect His character. The result is that they can stand firmly for truth and not be "tossed to and fro, and carried about with every wind of doctrine." There is nothing magical about these people—they are simply sinners that have been redeemed by the blood of the Lamb and who have learned how to trust and obey Jesus consistently, in every situation. Pray today that God will complete His work among His people. Pray that you will be among this group, and that your life will reflect the "fullness of Christ" to those around you.

Sample Prayer

Dear Father in heaven, the Bible promises that You will have a faithful and obedient people on this earth that reflect the character of Jesus Christ. I want to be among that group of people! Please complete Your work in me today, and every day, and give me victory over the sins and temptations that continue to separate me from You. Thank you for promising me strength through faith in Jesus Christ.

Reflection

_____

_____

_____

Final Thought

 The prince of this world cometh," said Jesus, "and hath nothing in Me." John 14:30. There was in Him nothing that responded to Satan's sophistry. He did not consent to sin. Not even by a thought did He yield to temptation. So it may be with us. Christ's humanity was united with divinity; He was fitted for the conflict by the indwelling of the Holy Spirit. And He came to make us partakers of the divine nature. So long as we are united to Him by faith, sin has no more dominion over us. God reaches for the hand of faith in us to direct it to lay fast hold upon the divinity of Christ, that we may attain to perfection of character.

The Desire of Ages, p. 123

Day 30

Prayer for a Finished Work

"And this gospel of the kingdom shall be preached in all the world for a witness unto all nations; and then shall the end come."

Matthew 24:14

Why hasn't Jesus come back yet? This question has hung on the lips of Christians since the day that Jesus ascended back to heaven, nearly 2,000 years ago. It can be tempting to compare the negative and shocking news headlines of today with the Bible's descriptions of the last days and to conclude that perhaps evil hasn't quite yet reached its fulfillment. This may be true; however, Jesus made it clear that His second coming is not dependent so much on the maturity of evil as it is on the maturity of His people. He will not return until His work among them is complete, and when that happens, they will be enabled to preach the gospel "in all the world for a witness unto all nations." Then the end will come. Pray today that Jesus will complete His work among His people, and that the church will come to character maturity through faith and obedience to His Word. Pray that the gospel will be proclaimed—through word and action—to the entire world. Pray that you, your family, and your church will be part of finishing this work. Pray that your community will respond to the gospel and be saved.

Sample Prayer

Dear Father in heaven, I pray today for myself, my family, and my church. I pray that we all may reflect the character of Christ, and love the people in our community as You do. I pray that the everlasting gospel and the Three Angels' Messages will be shared by word and action in my life and in the lives of my family members and church members. I pray for my community, that they may recognize You and Your truth as we share the gospel, and I pray that they will be saved.

Reflection

_____

_____

_____

_____

_____

Final Thought

Long has God waited for the spirit of service to take possession of the whole church so that everyone shall be working for Him according to his ability. When the members of the church of God do their appointed work in the needy fields at home and abroad, in fulfillment of the gospel commission, the whole world will soon be warned and the Lord Jesus will return to this earth with power and great glory. "This gospel of the kingdom shall be preached in all the world for a witness unto all nations; and then shall the end come." Matthew 24:14.

Acts of the Apostles, p. 111

Made in the USA
Monee, IL
18 October 2023

44748457R00049